POCAHONTAS AND THE STRANGERS

Clyde Robert Bulla

Illustrated by Peter Burchard
Cover illustration by Angelo Tillery

SCHOLASTIC INC.

New York   Toronto   London   Auckland   Sydney
Mexico City   New Delhi   Hong Kong   Buenos Aires

To Lenora Mattingly Weber,
friend and mentor

ISBN-13: 978-0-590-43481-2
ISBN-10: 0-590-43481-0

36 35 34   12/0
Printed in the U.S.A.   40

1

✦✦✦ *THE EAGLE* ✦✦✦

The boy and girl moved softly through the shadow of the woods. Each carried a bow and a quiver of arrows.

The boy was tall. The girl's head came only to his shoulder. Both were slim and straight. Their skin was the color of copper, and their long, black hair hung down their backs.

A squirrel sat up in the path ahead.

The boy put an arrow to his bow. He drew back the string and let it go with a twang. The shot missed. The squirrel disappeared among the bushes.

The boy stood still for a moment. He said, "Pick up the arrow."

The girl picked it up.

The boy was looking at her. His eyes were narrow. "Why did you laugh?" he asked.

"Laugh? I?" she said.

"You laughed because I missed the squirrel," he said.

"Oh, no, brother!" she said.

"You did. I saw you," he said. "Go back to the village."

"Don't send me home, Nantaquas," she said. "If I laughed it was because—because the woods are so green. It was because the flowers are in bloom again. It was because I am so glad to be hunting with you—"

"Stop," said the boy. "It is always this way. You make speeches as long as our father's."

He started on. She followed him. Her feet, in their deerskin moccasins, made hardly a sound, but he heard her.

"Pocahontas!" he said. "Go home!"

"Let me stay," she said. "You may shoot more game than you can carry. Then you will need me. Remember when you shot the turkeys and I helped carry them?"

He walked on. Again she followed him. This time he did not send her back.

She kept a few steps behind him. She looked up into the trees. The leaves were new. Bits of blue showed between the branches. All through the woods there was a kind of whisper.

She wanted to ask, "Do you hear the whisper? Where does it come from?" But it was not yet time to talk to her brother. He was still angry.

They came to a stream. He leaped across.

She could not jump so far. She ran along the stream until she came to a rock rising out of the water. She jumped to the rock, then on across.

Nantaquas had gone ahead. It took her a little while to find him. He was standing in an open space among the trees. On the ground in front of him sat a great brown bird. Its beak curved sharply downward. Its feathers were golden where the sun touched them.

Pocahontas gazed at the bird. Never before had she been so close to a live eagle.

She waited for it to fly. It spread its wings, but it did not rise. Then she saw why. Its feet were caught in a snare.

Nantaquas said, "I can take it alive."

"Who set the snare?" asked Pocahontas.

"How should I know?" he said.

"If the snare is not yours, you must not take the bird," she said.

"It must be taken now or not at all," he said. "The snare could not hold this bird for long."

The eagle lifted its head. The feathers ruffled about its neck.

"Look," said Pocahontas. "There is fire in its eyes." She said suddenly, "Nantaquas, let the bird go free."

He stared at her. "Let it go *free?* Our father will give me many presents for this bird. He will keep it in a cage. When it is older, its head and tail will turn white, and it will be a sight for everyone to see."

"You know what happens to birds in cages," she said. "They breathe the smoke of the house. They grow sleepy and die. The eagle will die, too."

"Then its head and wings will make a headdress for our father," said Nantaquas. "Stay and keep watch while I find a forked stick."

"What for?" she asked.

"To hold the eagle's head while you bind its legs," he told her.

As soon as he was gone, she waved her arms at the eagle. "Fly away," she said. "You could break free if you tried."

The snare was of knotted grass. It had been set between a bush and a tree. She gave the bush a shake. The bird opened and closed its beak, but it did not try to fly.

Pocahontas looked swiftly toward the place where she had last seen Nantaquas. He was not in sight.

She took an arrow from her quiver. With the edge of the arrowhead she cut through the snare.

"Fly!" she said.

The eagle screamed deep in its throat. It beat the air with its wings.

Nantaquas came running. He had a forked stick in his hand. He dropped the stick. He seized his bow and an arrow, but he was too late.

The eagle was already high off the ground. It screamed again. It went swooping off through the woods.

Nantaquas said to Pocahontas, "Is this how you keep watch?" He bent over the snare. "It was cut!" he said.

He came toward her. His hand was raised. She waited for the blow, but he did not strike.

"Pocahontas, hear what I say," he said in a cold, hard voice. "You can never hunt with me again."

She stood there for a while after he had gone. She had done wrong, she knew, yet she was not sorry the bird was free. She was only sorry that Nantaquas was angry.

Slowly she turned toward home.

She came to the high wall of poles that had been set up around the village. She went in through the open gateway.

The village was quiet. A few children and dogs played in the dust. Women had gathered under the beech tree. They were talking, with their heads together. There were no men in sight.

Pocahontas went toward the house of her father. He was Powhatan, king of the tribe and many other tribes as well. His house was the longest and largest in the village. The rounded roof was of reeds woven tightly enough to keep out the rain. The sides were of bark stripped from oak trees. Powhatan lived in the long house with his wives and many children.

Pocahontas looked inside. No one was there.

She started toward the house next to her father's— the council house, where the men held their meetings.

Her mother called to her, "Do not go in."

She was one of the women under the beech tree. "The men are inside," she said. "There is a meeting."

"Why?" asked Pocahontas.

"Have you not heard?" said her mother. "Three great canoes have come. They have wings that catch the wind—"

Pocahontas said, "The pale-faced men!"

"Yes," said her mother. "The pale-faced men are here."

2

Pocahontas looked about her.

"They are not in the village," said her mother. "Their canoes are in the bay."

"Comochok saw them," said another woman. "He ran all night to tell us."

"He brought a knife that came from the palefaces," said someone else. "It was like no other knife I ever saw."

As long as she could remember, Pocahontas had heard stories of the pale-faced men.

They rode the seas in great canoes. They covered themselves with clothing until only their hands and faces could be seen. They shot birds and deer and other animals with fire sticks that made a noise like thunder. All these were stories she had heard.

She had asked her father, "Are they real, the pale-faced men?"

"They are real," he had said, but he would tell her no more. It was plain that he did not want to talk about them.

She had asked the old ones of the tribe, "Have you seen the pale-faced men?"

Old Bekbek said he had seen them. But sometimes he told her they came out of the sea, and sometimes he said they lived on the moon. His stories were never the same.

Old Hapsis said she had seen the palefaces when she was young. Pocahontas almost believed her, although others said, "Her stories are only dreams. She is old and a little crazy."

The women under the beech tree were still talking. Pocahontas listened, but they were saying the same things over and over.

She looked toward the house where the men were

meeting. She knew her father would not punish her if she went inside. He never punished her. But she was sure he would not let her stay. He would only set her outside as if she were a puppy.

She went through the village, looking for someone to talk with. She came to Hapsis' wigwam.

The old woman was sitting in the doorway. The sun was on her wrinkled face. She sang to herself, as she rocked back and forth.

"Have you heard?" asked Pocahontas. "The palefaces have come."

"The palefaces?" said Hapsis. "I saw them."

"Where?" asked Pocahontas.

"Far from here," said the old woman, "and long ago."

Pocahontas knelt in front of the wigwam. "Tell me about them," she said.

"No," said the old woman. "You only laugh at me."

"I have never laughed at you," said Pocahontas. "Tell me again. Tell me about these men."

"There were women, too," said Hapsis. "I saw them in their village. It was far to the south. That was long before I came to this tribe."

"Did you talk with the palefaces?" asked Pocahontas.

"It was hard to talk with them. I did not know their words. They did not know mine," said the old woman, "but we learned from one another."

"What were their words like?" asked Pocahontas.

"They had a name for our people," said Hapsis. "They called us 'Indians.' Their name for our land was 'Virginia.' "

" 'In-dians,' " said Pocahontas. " 'Virgin-ia.' "

"They called themselves 'Englishmen,' " said Hapsis. "The name of their land was 'England.' "

"Was this land on the moon?" asked Pocahontas.

"No, no. It was across the great waters," said the old woman. "They came here and waited for others to come. While they waited, many of them died. They were sick and hungry."

"Hungry?" said Pocahontas. "Surely there was food here."

"They did not know how to find it," said Hapsis. "They tried to take our food. This made our chief angry. He and our men drove them out."

"Where did they go?" asked Pocahontas.

"Some were killed," said Hapsis. "Others were lost in the forest. Some may yet be alive, but I think not."

"Why did they leave their land across the sea?" asked Pocahontas. "Why did they come here?"

"Who knows?" said the old woman. "Whatever the reason, I think no more will ever come."

"They *have* come. You were not listening to me," said Pocahontas. "Their canoes are in the bay."

"What?" cried the old woman.

"They are here," said Pocahontas. "The palefaces have come in three canoes."

"We must hide," said Hapsis.

"Why?" asked Pocahontas.

"There is danger," said Hapsis.

"Why should there be danger?" asked Pocahontas.

"You are only a little child or you would not ask," said Hapsis.

"I am not a little child," said Pocahontas. "I have seen eleven summers, and I know many things. My father says I—"

"Listen," said the old woman. The men were talking, as they came out of the council house. "What do they say?"

Pocahontas went to her father.

Powhatan was a tall man. IIis hair was gray. There were deep lines in his cheeks and forehead.

"What will you do, now that the palefaces are here?" Pocahontas asked him. "What did you say at the meeting?"

"Must you know everything?" he said.

He wore a necklace of bear claws. She caught hold of it and tried to pull his head down to hers. "*Tell* me," she said. "I have to know!"

"I'll tell you, then," he said. "We are going to wait. Before we do anything, we are going to see what the palefaces do. There, I have told you. Now go and play."

He was smiling, yet she felt that he was anxious. She began to feel anxious, too.

Long past bedtime little groups sat on the river bank outside the village. They talked in low voices.

Pocahontas saw Nantaquas sitting alone. She crept up beside him.

"Comochok brought a knife from the palefaces," she said. "Did you see it?"

He did not answer.

"I talked with Hapsis today," she said. "She told me the story again—how she went to the palefaces' village and learned to talk with them."

"She talks too much," said Nantaquas, "and so do you."

Pocahontas was happy. He had spoken to her. Now she knew that he was no longer angry.

He let her sit beside him. They listened to the fish jump in the river. They watched the stars on the water.

3

"Long ago the canoes of the palefaces came here and went away. These, too, will go away." This was the talk in the village.

But the palefaces stayed. Their great canoes moved in and out of the streams that flowed into the bay.

Every day Pocahontas climbed high into the beech tree. From there she could see far down the river. She watched for the palefaces. "Why do they not come *here?*" she kept asking.

"You will bring them no faster by sitting in the tree," said her mother. "Come down. There is work to do."

The women and older girls were busy in the fields near the village. They had planted squash and pumpkin seeds. They had planted corn and beans. Now the squash and pumpkin vines were covering the ground. The corn was growing tall, and bean vines were climbing the stalks.

The women and girls bent their backs in the fields. They pulled weeds or chopped them out with hoes. Pocahontas worked with the others.

The men's life was easy, she thought. Every day they hunted and fished and watched the palefaces.

Powhatan had sent his spies all the way to the bay. They hid among the rocks and trees. Day and night they watched.

One evening the warrior Comochok brought news. He sat with Powhatan outside the king's house and they talked together.

Comochok said, "The palefaces are on shore. They are cutting trees and building houses."

"Where?" asked Powhatan.

"A half-day's walk from here," the warrior told him, "on a finger of land that points into the river."

"Where the river bends like this?" Powhatan made a mark on the ground with a stick.

"Yes," said Comochok.

"Surely they are foolish to build houses there," said Powhatan. "The land is low and wet. It is a place of flies and mosquitoes."

"But the water is deep there," said Comochok. "They can bring their great canoes close to the shore."

Pocahontas had been listening in the doorway.

"Father," she said.

"Yes, my daughter," said Powhatan.

"I want to see the palefaces," she said. "I want to go with Comochok and see everything he sees."

Powhatan said to Comochok, "You have heard. Here is someone to walk beside you. Her eyes are sharp, and she can run like a rabbit. But when she is tired, you must carry her on your back like a papoose."

"I need no one to carry me!" said Pocahontas. "I can walk as far and as fast as anyone else, and I want to go—"

"No, my daughter. I need you here." Powhatan gave her a little push. "Run and play now. Leave us to our talk."

She walked through the village.

Near the gate she met Nantaquas.

"Why do you walk with your head down?" he asked. "Why do you kick up the dust?"

She frowned at him.

"What troubles you?" he asked.

"They laugh at me," she said.

"Who?" asked Nantaquas.

"Father and Comochok," she said. "I want to see the palefaces. I asked to go with Comochok, and they laughed."

"Father wants no harm to come to you," said Nantaquas.

"What harm could come to me? I could watch the palefaces without being seen," she said.

"Their canoes are not always in the same place," he said. "Where would you go to find them?"

"I know where to go," she said. "Comochok says they are building houses only a half-day's walk from here. Nantaquas, let us go see!"

"No," he said.

"No one will miss us if we go now," she said.

"It is too late to start today," he said. "A half-day's walk, you say? We could not get there and back before dark."

"Tomorrow, then," she said.

"We should wait," he said, "until father says—"

She broke in, "I am going tomorrow. Meet me early by the south cornfield. If you are not there, I shall go alone."

Early in the morning she went to the south cornfield. Nantaquas was waiting.

4

They kept near the river. They found a path and followed it.

Pocahontas walked behind Nantaquas. Sometimes they ran.

If they came home in daylight, no one would ask where they had been. If they were later than sundown, their father would ask, "Where did you go? What did you do?" He would look at them in such a way that they would have to tell the truth.

They lost the path in a thicket of oaks and grape-vines.

"Tell me again," said Nantaquas. "What did Comochok say?"

"A half-day's walk from our village," she said. "A finger of land that points into the river."

They took another path and followed it a long way. Nantaquas lay down and drank from a little stream. Pocahontas drank beside him. She lay there, listening.

"What is that?" she asked.

It was a hammering sound, sharp and heavy.

"A drum?" he said.

"Surely more than one," she said.

He put his ear to the ground and listened. "I do not think they are drums," he said.

They went toward the sound. Voices began to come to them. She tried to listen.

"Keep down," said Nantaquas.

He was crawling like a snake. She crept after him.

They were in the tall weeds at the edge of the woods. He parted the weeds and looked out. She looked over his shoulder. She saw the low strip of land along the river. The palefaces were there.

They looked like dark bundles of clothing. Only their hands and faces showed. She wondered how they could move in so many clothes.

But they did move, and quickly, too. Some were chopping down trees. Their axes made the sounds Pocahontas and Nantaquas had heard.

Others were cutting through tree trunks with long, black bands. Two men pulled each band back and forth.

A tree fell, then another.

Once Pocahontas had seen her brothers bring down a tree. They had set fire to the trunk, then chopped away the burned part with their stone hatchets. They had burned and chopped again and again. It had taken many days.

But the palefaces' axes bit into the wood and only a few blows brought a tree crashing down.

She looked beyond, to the finger of land that pointed out into the river. It was almost an island. The palefaces were building houses there.

Three great canoes were tied to trees on the river bank. She would not have believed a canoe could be so large. In the smallest one there was room for everyone in her village.

Some of the men walked about with long, black sticks in their hands. One of them lifted a stick to his shoulder. There was a noise like thunder. Smoke and fire came from the end of the stick.

Pocahontas lay close to the ground.

"Look!" she heard Nantaquas say.

She raised her head and looked. The man was picking a bird up off the ground. He was holding it by a wing.

She wanted to ask Nantaquas, "Is it true? Did he kill the bird with his firestick?" But she said nothing. Two men were coming near.

"Do not move," whispered Nantaquas.

The men were looking at something on the ground. It was a small stone. They seemed to be talking about it. Their voices were low and pleasant.

They came closer. They were on their hands and knees, picking up more stones. Their faces were almost covered with thick reddish hair. Their noses were short. Their skin was pale, but not white like the paint the warriors put on their faces.

One of the men said something. They both laughed, and she saw the flash of their teeth.

They stood up and moved on. More trees fell. Men were walking across a kind of bridge from one of the great canoes to the shore. They were carrying loads on their backs.

"What do they have?" asked Pocahontas.

"I do not know," answered Nantaquas. "Come. We must not stay any longer."

They took the path toward the village.

Many questions came to Pocahontas. Who were the pale-faced strangers? Why were they here? Had they truly come from across the sea?

Nantaquas spoke. "The firesticks are stronger than bows and arrows." That was all he said on the way home.

Back in the village, no one asked where they had been. People were talking in great excitement.

"Did you see how they looked at us?" someone said.

"They gave me these beads," said a girl.

"Who?" asked Pocahontas.

"The palefaces," said the girl.

"They were *here*?" asked Pocahontas.

"Yes—yes!" said the girl.

"It is a pity you were away," said Pocahontas' mother. "You could have seen them."

"They came up the river in one of their canoes," said Comochok. "It was a big canoe, but not a *very* big one."

"They are ugly, with their pale skin and fox-eyes," said a woman.

"They are strange, but not ugly," said Pocahontas.

"How do you know?" said the woman. "You were not here."

And Pocahontas said no more.

5

✛✛✛ *THE HUNTERS* ✛✛✛

The next day Pocahontas' older brother, Parahunt, came to the village. Her uncle, Opekankano, was with him. They were chiefs in their own villages. Powhatan was king over all.

The three men met in the council house.

Pocahontas asked Nantaquas, "Why do they meet?"

"To talk of war," he answered. "They mean to drive out the palefaces."

"How can this be?" she said. "Our father says they are our friends."

"He does not always say so," said Nantaquas.

"Why should he make war on the palefaces?" she asked.

"Because of what he hears," said Nantaquas. "He hears that the palefaces mean to make war on us."

Days went by, Pocahontas saw no signs of war. But sometimes the warriors talked together in a way that was secret and strange.

One night she woke and heard footsteps outside the house. She heard the gate open and close.

In the morning she told her father, "Someone left the village last night."

"My daughter's ears are sharp," he said. "Yes, some of the men left early. They are going far from here to hunt."

"Will they bring back a bear?" she asked.

"They may," he said.

"Will you give the skin to me?" she asked. "I need it for my bed."

"If they bring back a bear, you shall have the skin," he promised.

Pocahontas was happy. She went to where two of her younger sisters were playing under the beech tree. "The hunters may bring back a bear," she told them, "and I am to have the skin for my bed."

She played with her sisters in the cool shade. She made them rings and necklaces of grass.

They swung on the grapevine swings outside the village. They played until the women and girls came out to the fields.

Pocahontas worked with them. In the afternoon she helped them weave grass into a large fishing net.

Just after sunset she heard the splash of paddles in the river.

"The hunters!" she said, and she went to stand by the gate.

Two canoes came to shore. Men got out and walked past her. Some of them limped as if they had been hurt. They spoke to no one as they went into the village and into the council house.

They had not brought a bear. They had brought no meat of any kind.

It was strange, she thought. They had hunted all day and brought back nothing.

She spoke of this to Nantaquas the next morning.

"They brought no meat," he said, "because they did not go hunting."

"Where *did* they go?" she asked.

"If I tell you," he said, "do you promise to tell no one?"

"I promise," she said.

Nantaquas said, "Our men met with warriors from other tribes. They all went to fight the palefaces and burn their houses and canoes."

"How do you know this?" she asked.

"Comochok's brother told me," said Nantaquas. "The warriors surprised the palefaces, but the palefaces fought back. They had great firesticks on their canoes. They shot them into the trees. Branches came off the trees and fell among the warriors, and they turned and ran."

"If all this is true," said Pocahontas, "why did our father not tell us? Why did he pretend the men were going hunting?"

"Our father is wise," said Nantaquas. "He sent our men in secret. Now if the palefaces come here with their firesticks, he can still say we are friends. He can say the men who made war were from another tribe."

"Is he afraid of the palefaces?" she asked.

"He is afraid of no one," said Nantaquas.

"Then why should he pretend to be their friend when he is not?" she asked.

"I have told you," said Nantaquas. "Our father is a wise man. You cannot understand these things. You are only a foolish girl!"

6

The palefaces were building more houses. They had put up a wall between their village and the woods. Their great canoes were gone, but most of the men had stayed.

This was the news brought to Powhatan.

"Go to them," the king told Comochok. "Find out what you can."

Comochok went to the palefaces' village. He took a deer and a turkey he had shot. He made a sign that he wanted to trade them for a firestick.

The palefaces would not give him a firestick. Instead

they traded hoes, axes, and beads for the deer and the turkey.

Pocahontas asked for one of the axes. Her father gave it to her. She liked the feel of the smooth, hard metal.

Many times that summer Comochok went to trade with the palefaces. Other men went with him. They began to learn the palefaces' language.

"Teach me," said Pocahontas, and one day Comochok sat with her outside the king's house and told her the words he knew. "English" was one. The palefaces were English. They came from a land called England.

"This is what Hapsis told me long ago," she said. "Do the English call us Indians?"

"Yes," answered Comochok.

"Do they call this land Virginia?" she asked.

"Yes," said Comochok, "and the name of their village is Jamestown. James is the king of England. Jamestown means the village of the king of England."

"Did you see the king?" asked Pocahontas.

"He does not live here," Comochok told her.

"Do these men have no chief?" she asked.

"I do not know," said Comochok. "I talked with one

who is a little like a chief. He often tells the others what to do. His name is Captain John Smith."

Powhatan had come out of the house. "This Captain John Smith," he asked "is he tall?"

Comochok held up his hand. "His head comes this high."

"Then he is not so tall as I. Is he young or old?" asked Powhatan.

"Younger than you," said Comochok.

"Then he cannot be so wise as I," said Powhatan, and he looked pleased.

He looked pleased, too, when he heard that there was trouble in Jamestown.

"The palefaces often quarrel," said one of the warriors.

"They do not have enough to eat," said another. "They raise no crops, and they know little of hunting and fishing. They brought food from their homeland, but it is nearly gone."

Early in the winter came the news that brought a look of joy to Powhatan's face.

A man from Opekankano's village brought the story.

Some of the palefaces had gone up the river to find food. Opekankano's men had seized three of them. Two they had killed. The third they had taken prisoner. He was Captain John Smith.

"We shall see how great a chief he is," said Powhatan.

The paleface was shown in Opekankano's village. Then he was taken to another village, and another and another. Each time he was shown there was a feast, and many people gathered. They looked at the paleface. They touched his skin and his clothing. They watched him eat.

"When he is brought here," said Powhatan, "our feast will be the biggest of all."

The feast day came. Opekankano had sent runners the evening before. The prisoner was on the way, they said.

The men oiled and painted themselves. They put on their robes and feathers and beads. Women and children, too, painted themselves and dressed in their best.

Pocahontas wore her feather robe. It was made of

small, soft turkey feathers. It was light, yet warm. She wrapped it about her and waited for Captain John Smith.

She was at the gate when Opekankano and his warriors came out of the woods. They walked in a long line. In the middle of the line was the paleface.

His hands were tied behind him. He walked as if he were tired.

Opekankano greeted Pocahontas.

"Welcome, uncle," she said.

Captain John Smith raised his head. She saw his face. It was half covered with golden hair. His eyes were blue. Never before had she seen a man's eyes that were blue.

He was looking at her. He seemed about to speak. Then he and the other men went on into the village.

Pocahontas felt warm. She felt happy. The paleface had looked at her. She was almost sure he had smiled.

She wanted to smile back. She wanted to hear his voice.

She started after the men. Before she could overtake them, they had gone into the council house.

Old Hapsis looked out of her wigwam. "Is the pale-face here?" she asked.

"Yes. I saw him." Pocahontas went in and sat by the old woman's fire. "His hair is gold, and his eyes are—but you will see him at the feast tonight."

"Not I," said Hapsis.

"Everyone will be there," said Pocahontas.

"I shall not go," said the old woman.

"Even some from other tribes are coming," said Pocahontas. "You must be there."

"No," said Hapsis. "I have seen enough of killing."

Pocahontas said quickly, "They will not kill the pale-face!"

"Yes," said Hapsis. "Oh, yes, they will."

"How do you know?" asked Pocahontas. "Who told you?"

"No one had to tell me," said the old woman. "Is he not the chief of the palefaces?"

"He may be one of the chiefs," said Pocahontas.

"Our men say he is the leader," said Hapsis. "Your father does not trust them. If the leader is gone, it will be easier to drive the rest away."

Pocahontas said, "It would be wrong to kill the pale-face."

"Are you wiser than your father?" asked Hapsis.

"In this one way I may be," said Pocahontas.

"Your words are bold," said the old woman, "but you do nothing."

"That is true," said Pocahontas. "I do nothing."

Hapsis was watching the girl's face. "Yet there is something you might do."

"What is that?" asked Pocahontas.

"There is the law of the tribe," said the old woman. "If a prisoner is to be killed, a woman may say, 'Give me this man. He is mine.' Then the man must be set free and given to her."

Pocahontas said slowly, "I have never seen this. I have never seen a woman ask for a prisoner."

"All the same, it is the law," said Hapsis.

"I am not a woman," said Pocahontas. "I am only a girl."

"You are the king's daughter," said Hapsis. "He gives you what you ask for."

Pocahontas looked into the fire. After a while she

said, "I do not think the paleface will be killed. I think my father means only to have a feast and let everyone see him."

"You may think as you please," said the old woman, and she, too, sat looking into the fire.

7

Pocahontas and her mother went to the feast. The council house was crowded. Powhatan was sitting high on a throne made of poles and mats. Two of his young wives sat beside him.

About the throne stood four tall warriors. They were Powhatan's guards. Each held a blazing torch, and the council house was filled with flickering light.

Women moved through the crowd. They carried wooden platters of food—roasted deer meat, corn cakes, potatoes, and pieces of squash. Some of the women were pouring cups of the white brew they had made of water and crushed hickory nuts.

Pocahontas and her mother found places near the throne. Other wives of Powhatan sat there, and many of Powhatan's children. Before them a circle had been marked out on the floor. The circle was empty.

"That is for the paleface," said Pocahontas' mother.

"Where is he now?" asked Pocahontas.

"In another house," said her mother. "He will not be here until after we have feasted. We do not feast with our enemy."

"Is he our enemy?" asked Pocahontas.

"Yes, I think so," answered her mother.

"Will they kill him?" asked Pocahontas.

"Your father will say," answered her mother.

Music began to play. Along with the drumbeats were the high notes of a reed pipe. Pocahontas could not see the men who were playing. She thought they were outside.

She took a piece of deer meat when it was passed to her. She held it to her mouth and pretended to eat. She was not hungry.

When the feast was over, women brought bowls of water and handfuls of feathers. The people washed their hands in the water and dried them on the feathers.

There was a noise in the doorway. The music stopped. Everyone stopped talking.

Two warriors had come into the council house. They were leading the paleface between them. They led him to the empty circle and gave him a push.

His legs were bound together. His hands were tied behind his back. He fell like a log of wood. Powhatan was smiling, and some of the warriors laughed aloud.

The paleface lay in the dust. A man untied his hands. The prisoner sat up.

Women brought him food. He ate quickly. When he had finished, a woman brought him water and feathers. He dipped his fingers into the bowl and splashed a little water on his forehead. He dried his hands and face on the feathers.

Only then did he look about him. He looked from one face to another.

Powhatan began to speak. "Has this paleface done us harm? Has he? Who can tell how this paleface has done us harm?"

An old man spoke. "Who asked the palefaces to

come here? We did not ask them, yet they have come and built their houses. Next they will take our homes and shoot us down with their firesticks."

A small girl moved close to Pocahontas. She was Mattachanna, one of Pocahontas' sisters.

"I wore all my beads," she whispered.

"Be quiet, so I can hear," said Pocahontas.

"It is no matter," said the little girl. "They are only talking."

"Be quiet," said Pocahontas.

Other men spoke. Each one said the same—that the paleface was their enemy.

"Then," said Powhatan, "he shall die."

"No!" cried Pocahontas. She sprang up. "Father—"

Powhatan looked down at her. "Keep back," he said.

"Keep back," said someone else, and she was pushed aside.

Two warriors came forward. Each carried a large, flat stone. They put the stones down in the circle.

Again they tied the prisoner's hands behind his back. They rolled him over until his head was on the stones.

The people were shouting. They pressed closer to the circle.

Two more warriors came forward. Each carried a heavy wooden club. They stood over the prisoner. He lay on his back and looked up at them. There was no sign of fear in his eyes.

The warriors raised their clubs.

"No!" cried Pocahontas. She threw herself down upon the prisoner. She put her head upon his.

Now the men could not strike the paleface without striking her.

Hands seized her. They tried to pull her away. She held to the prisoner.

A man was shouting angry words. He was a warrior from another tribe. He caught her by the hair.

Her father said in a loud voice, "Do not harm her. She is my daughter."

The man let go of her hair.

She raised her head. The men were still standing over her with their clubs. She said to her father, "Give me this man. He is mine."

Powhatan opened his mouth and closed it.

"I have asked for him. You must give him to me," she cried. "It is the law."

Powhatan made a sign for her to get up.

"First tell the men not to strike," she said.

"They will not strike," he said.

She stood beside the paleface. "Is he mine?" she asked. "Do you give him to me?"

"Why do you want him?" asked her father.

"He can do many things for us," she said. "He can—he can make beads and bells for me. He can teach us to make great canoes and firesticks. Father, say he is mine."

Powhatan sat with his chin in his hand.

She said again, "Father—"

"He is yours," said Powhatan.

Pocahontas untied the prisoner's arms and legs. "Now you are mine," she said.

He spoke. She could not understand his words.

He looked at the king, then at Pocahontas. He rose to his knees. He took both her hands in his and held them against his face.

8

✠✠✠ SON AND BROTHER ✠✠✠

Some in the tribe were angry. "This man is our enemy," they said. "The king should not have spared him." But they spoke softly so that Powhatan could not hear.

Others in the tribe were pleased. "Our king was wise to let the paleface live," they said. "If we are friends with him and his people, we can trade with them. We can use their axes and knives and firesticks."

The day after the feast, Powhatan and his warriors took Captain John Smith off into the woods.

They were gone all night. In the morning Pocahontas waited outside the village. She saw her father and the warriors coming through the trees. Their faces and arms were painted. They carried war-clubs and bows and arrows.

For a moment she was afraid. Then she saw him—Captain John Smith. He was walking among the warriors. He had not been harmed.

She went to meet him.

Powhatan was smiling. "I have brought him back to you," he said. "In the woods we held a ceremony. Now he is my son."

"Your son, my brother," said Pocahontas.

The paleface picked her up and carried her into the village.

People crowded about them.

"Leave me with my brother," she said.

She slipped out of his arms. She led him to the council house.

Inside the house they were alone. They sat on mats by the fire.

He talked to her. He knew some words in her language. He made her understand that he was cold and tired.

She put more wood on the fire. She brought a sleeping-mat.

He lay on the mat. Almost at once he was asleep.

She looked down at his face. There were deep lines in his forehead. There were dark patches under his eyes.

He is not young, she thought.

Yet when his short sleep was over, he looked almost young again. His eyes were clear and bright. He sat up straight on the mat.

He tried to speak in her language.

"Teach me *your* words," she said. "I know some. Listen. 'Indian'—'English'—'Virginia.' Teach me more."

He taught her to say, " 'I am Pocahontas. I am an Indian.' " He taught her, " 'You are Captain John Smith. You are an Englishman.' "

From inside his coat he took a scrap of something as thin as a leaf. "Paper," he said.

He took a stick of charcoal from the fire. With the end of the stick he made marks on the paper.

He showed her the marks. " 'Captain John Smith,' " he said.

She was puzzled.

He said again, " 'Captain John Smith.' " He pointed to the marks, then to himself.

She began to understand that he had a way of putting his name down on the paper.

She pointed to herself, then to the marks. "Make my name," she said.

There was no more room on the paper.

She brought some pieces of birchbark. He took one of them and made a few marks across it. " 'Pocahontas,' " he said.

She took the birchbark. With another piece of charcoal she tried to copy her name. It was not easy to do. Halfway through, she rubbed out what she had done.

She drew a picture instead. She drew a house.

"My house," she told him.

He drew a house with a roof that came to a peak. "English house," he said.

He began to draw on another piece of bark. He made a crooked line.

"What is that?" she asked.

"River," he said.

He made a dot. "Indian village," he said. He made another dot. "Jamestown."

He held up the birchbark. "Map," he said.

"Map," she said after him. "I can make a map, too!"

Powhatan came into the council house. He had brought a pipe of tobacco to smoke with Captain John Smith.

"We are making maps," Pocahontas told him. "See? Here is the river—"

"Put it aside," said Powhatan. "Have you not talked long enough together—you and your brother, Captain John Smith?"

"No," she said. "I could never be tired of talking with Captain John Smith."

"There are others who wish to see him," said her father. "I, too, wish to talk with him before he goes."

"Before he *goes?*" she said.

"Back to Jamestown," he told her.

"He is not going." cried Pocahontas. "He is mine. You said so—you gave him to me!"

"Would you keep him beside you always?" asked Powhatan.

"Yes!" she said.

"Listen to what I say," he began.

"No! You promised me!" The map slipped off her knees and into the fire. She reached for it, but the dry bark was already blazing. Tears came to her eyes.

"Pocahontas—" said her father.

She turned her face away. She was ashamed of her tears.

"I gave the paleface to you. He is yours wherever he goes," said Powhatan. "He must be free to go to Jamestown. His people wait for him there. When he comes to us again, he will bring gifts."

"How do you know he will come back?" she asked.

"Is he not my son now?" said Powhatan. "Is he not your brother?"

She thought for a while.

Captain John Smith spoke to her. She could not understand his words, but it seemed to her that he was saying, "Let me go."

"Yes," she said. "You must go. It is right. But do not forget"—she pointed to him, then to herself—"you are mine, and you must come back!"

9

In the morning Pocahontas was up early. She went to the council house. "Captain John Smith!" she called softly.

Her father looked out. "Captain John Smith is not here," he said.

"Where is he?" she asked. "I have come to guide him back to Jamestown."

"He has already gone," said Powhatan.

"Why did you let him go without me?" she asked. "He does not know the way. He will be lost."

"Twelve of our men have gone to guide him," said Powhatan.

"Twelve?" said Pocahontas. "Would not one have been enough?"

"He may send us gifts. It may take twelve men to carry them." He tried to put his hand on her head. "Do not look so angry. You said yourself that it was right for him to go."

"I did not say *when*," she said. "I was not ready for him to go. I am going to bring him back."

"When the warriors return," he said, "Captain John Smith may return with them."

"Do you think so?" she asked.

"It may be so," he said.

"Then," said Pocahontas, "I had better wait."

Toward evening she saw the twelve men come into the village. They did not look happy.

Comochok carried a string of beads and a few of the palefaces' knives. The other warriors' hands were empty.

Pocahontas asked them, "Where is Captain John Smith?"

The men would not talk to her. They went on into the council house where Powhatan waited for them.

The next day Pocahontas learned what had happened. Comochok told her. She sat down near him outside his house. She watched while he skinned the deer he had killed.

"Where is Captain John Smith?" she asked.

"In Jamestown, for all I know," said Comochok. "That is where we left him."

He told his story.

The twelve warriors had taken Captain John Smith to Jamestown. There he gave them two great firesticks called cannon. He gave them a great round stone for grinding grain.

The cannon and the stone were very heavy. The warriors could not carry them.

Some of the men grew angry. "The palefaces are laughing at us," they said.

"Why do you frown? I have given you good presents," said Captain John Smith, and he said he would show them how to shoot the cannon.

There was a large tree near the river. Its branches were covered with ice. Captain John Smith shot at the tree. Smoke and fire came out of the cannon, and there was a noise that shook the earth. Half the tree was shot away, and branches and ice came tumbling down.

The warriors put their hands to their ears. They ran into the woods.

Captain John Smith came after them. He told them not to be afraid.

He led them back to Jamestown and gave them a few presents that they could carry home.

Pocahontas asked Comochok, "Why did he not come with you?"

"He had to care for his men," answered Comochok. "Some were ill, and all were hungry."

"Hungry?" said Pocahontas. "How can this be?"

"They know little of hunting or fishing," said Comochok. "Last summer they raised no crops, so they have no grain."

"I shall take them food," said Pocahontas.

She called the children together. "The palefaces are ill and hungry," she said. "We are going to take food to Jamestown."

They begged food from every house in the village. Still their baskets were not full.

Pocahontas opened one of the storehouses. From the store of food she took corn and beans.

Some of the people said to Powhatan, "See what your daughter is doing. You must stop her."

"There is enough food," he said. "Some good may come of this."

Pocahontas guided the children through the woods.

Some carried the heaviest baskets on poles between them. Others carried baskets on their heads.

The little streams were frozen. They walked across on the ice.

They laughed and sang. They kicked up the leaves under their feet.

But when they came to Jamestown, most of the children were shy. They wanted to wait in the woods.

"No, you must come with me," said Pocahontas. "Captain John Smith will let no harm come to us."

She went up to the wall. It was made of logs set on end.

The gate opened. Captain John Smith came out. He looked as if he could not believe what he saw.

"We have brought food," she said.

"Pocahontas!" he said. "Once before you saved my life. Now you have come to save us all!"

10

✦✦✦ *A QUARREL* ✦✦✦

Every few days Pocahontas took food to Jamestown. Always Captain John Smith was there to welcome her.

"You are too good to us—you are too kind," he would say in his own language.

"Why should I not be kind to my brother?" she would answer in the language of her people. And somehow they would understand each other.

Each time they met she learned more of his words, and he learned more of hers.

She liked to walk with him among the houses of Jamestown. On every side there were strange and interesting things to see. Sometimes she stopped to look at a lantern or a piece of rope or clothing hung out to dry.

She asked about the clothing. "What animal skin is it made of?"

"It is cloth, not animal skin," John Smith told her. He spread his handkerchief out for her to see. He showed her how the threads were woven together.

He gave her a mirror. She asked how it happened that she could see herself in the glass.

She asked why his face was shaggy and her father's face was smooth.

"Pocahontas, stop!" he said. "You ask more questions than I can answer."

She watched the Englishmen building a house.

"Why do they make it so thick and heavy?" she asked.

"Houses must be strong," said Captain John Smith.

"But how can you move them?" she asked.

"Why should we move them?" he asked.

"We move our houses," she said. "We can take down the poles and mats and put them up somewhere else."

"Why?" he asked.

"If another place looks better, we move our houses," she told him.

"This is not the English way," he said. "We build our houses to stay."

"This is strange," she said.

She thought it strange, too, that there were no women and children in Jamestown.

"Life is hard for us here," he said. "It would be too hard for women and little ones. Before they come, we must have good houses and enough food."

A ship came from England. At first Pocahontas thought it had brought women and children, but it had brought only men.

The ship's captain was Captain Newport. With him were fifty men who had come to live in Jamestown.

Pocahontas told her father about the captain.

"I wish to meet this man," said Powhatan. "Tell him I will trade with him."

Pocahontas took the message to Jamestown.

A few days later Captain John Smith and a party of men came to the village.

Pocahontas made them welcome.

"Newport will soon be here," said John Smith.

Powhatan came out to meet them. He shook his head when he saw that the men had brought their firesticks.

Pocahontas said to John Smith, "My father asks why you carry firesticks. Do you not trust us?"

"We always carry firesticks when we leave home," said John Smith. "Tell him it is our custom."

There was feasting that night in Powhatan's house. Pocahontas sat beside Captain John Smith, and he told her about England. He talked on and on about the beautiful lakes and rivers and castles and cities of his land.

"Will you take me there?" she asked.

"Yes," he said.

"When?" she asked.

"When I go, you shall go with me," he said.

The palefaces went to another wigwam to sleep. Pocahontas looked for Nantaquas. She found him lying on a mat in a corner.

"Brother," she said, "I am going away. I am going across the great sea."

He said nothing.

"Did you hear?" she asked. "When Captain John Smith goes to England, he will take me with him. He will show me all the lakes and rivers and castles and cities of his land."

"He told you this?" said Nantaquas.

"Yes," she said.

"And you believed him?"

"Why should I not believe him?" she asked.

"He is not truly your brother. These palefaces are not truly our friends," he said. "If they came as friends, they would not bring their firesticks into our village. Their Captain Newport does not trust us. That is why he sent John Smith before him—to make sure there was no danger."

"These are thoughts you made up in your own head," she said.

"These are things I know," he said. "Why do you think the English have left their land to come here? Because they want our land, too. They want it for themselves and their king. But I know you will not listen to me. You must learn for yourself."

"It is you who must learn!" she said, and she walked away.

Afterward she was sorry she had quarreled with Nantaquas. She took him a bowl of dried corn. But he would not eat it, and he turned his head away from her.

11

In the morning Captain Newport was there with twenty of his men. Captain Newport was a small man with a pink face. He kept smiling and nodding as if he were trying hard to be friendly.

For the next three days there was feasting in the village.

In Powhatan's house one night, Captain Newport made a speech: "Great king, I bring you a gift from my country. I bring you this man, Tom Savage, to be your servant. Day and night he will be near you."

He pushed one of his men forward.

Powhatan made a speech: "Mighty leader from

across the sea, this gift of friendship I give you in return. I give you my guard, Namontack. May he learn your ways and be your faithful servant."

Namontack came forward. He and Tom Savage stood side by side. Both men were young. Tom Savage had freckles and a snub nose. He looked scared, and his eyes moved from side to side. Namontack stood tall and straight. The light gleamed on his dark skin. He was smiling a little, and the look on his face never changed.

Pocahontas was sitting at her father's feet. Nantaquas was nearby, and she heard him whisper to one of their brothers, "These are only speeches that mean nothing. The palefaces will not leave one of their men. They will not take one of ours."

But when the English left, Namontack left with them. Tom Savage stayed behind.

The young Englishman wandered about the village. He looked awkward and afraid. Some of the warriors laughed at him.

Pocahontas spoke kindly to him.

Before many days they were talking together. He

was playing games and hunting with the other young men.

He said to Pocahontas, "I like it here, I do! When I heard the captain giving me away, I couldn't believe my own ears. I almost spoke up and said, 'See here, you can't do that.' But being a servant is easy here. The king doesn't need much done for him, and I spend my days eating and sleeping and keeping warm."

In Jamestown Namontack was not so happy.

Pocahontas talked with him there. He told her about the fire that had burned the town.

"A spark came from a chimney and fell on a roof," he said, "and everything burned. The English set me to work helping build the town again. All day I carry wood and stones. It is hard being a servant here."

Another time he told her, "These English are mad. They dig sand and put it into bags. They load the bags on the ships. What do they do with the sand?"

Pocahontas asked John Smith, "Why do you load your ships with sand? Have you none in England?"

"The men see something in the sand that shines," he said. "They think it is gold. I tell them it is not, but they do not believe me."

"Why do they want gold?" she asked.

"Gold is good to have," he said.

"Better than copper?" she asked.

"Oh, yes, Pocahontas," he said. "A man who has much gold is rich."

She remembered his words: "A man who has much gold is rich." She puzzled over them, but she could not understand them.

When spring came, Captain Newport sailed for England. Namontack sailed with him.

Some of the Englishmen worked on at building houses. Others planted fields of corn and beans just outside Jamestown.

"They have no pumpkin seeds," Pocahontas told her father, as they fished on the river bank one day. "Let us take them some. Let us go to Jamestown tomorrow, just you and I."

"I cannot go there," he said. "I am the king. The Englishmen must come to me."

"Then how can you see their houses?" she asked. "I want you to see them. They are strange."

"Captain Newport promised me an English house,"

said Powhatan. "He will send men here to build it when he comes back from England."

"He may be gone a long time," she said. "Let me talk with Captain John Smith. He will see that you have an English house."

"Captain John Smith? I do not think so," said Powhatan. "He takes everything and leaves me nothing. Each time we trade—"

He stopped. He was looking down the river. Three canoes were there.

They came to the landing. Men sprang out. One of them was Comochok. He began to talk to Powhatan, and his words came fast.

"There is trouble," he said. "The palefaces caught some of our men and beat them. Two are still prisoners at Jamestown."

Powhatan's eyes flashed. "Why have the palefaces done this?"

"Because," said Comochok, "some of our men tried to take firesticks and axes and other things from Jamestown."

"Captain Newport promised me these things," said Powhatan. "It is Captain John Smith who keeps them from us."

He started toward the village. The other men followed him.

Pocahontas watched them go. She was thinking, There will be war.

This would be like no war her people had ever known. This would be Powhatan's tribe against the English. It would be bows and arrows against firesticks.

She went up the path to the village. She did not go

to her father's house. She went instead to Hapsis' wigwam.

"Have you heard?" she asked the old woman.

"I have heard," answered Hapsis.

"I shall stay with you tonight," said Pocahontas. "I do not wish to hear the talking."

The next day went slowly. Pocahontas looked for painted warriors with shields and bows and arrows. She saw none.

Late in the day Comochok came to Hapsis' wigwam.

"A messenger is here from Jamestown," he said. "He is one of Opekankano's men. The palefaces met him in the woods and sent him here with a message from Captain John Smith."

"What message?" she asked.

"These are the words," said Comochok. "Captain John Smith says he will give up the prisoners if Pocahontas will come for them."

12

✦✦✦ THE PRISONERS ✦✦✦

Comochok and his friend Rawhunt took Pocahontas down the river in a canoe.

They came in sight of Jamestown. Englishmen with firesticks were guarding the wall.

"I will go no farther," said Rawhunt.

"Stop here, then, and wait for me," said Pocahontas.

The men pulled over to the shore. She climbed out. She walked through the fields the Englishmen had planted. Corn and beans were up, but weeds were thick in the rows.

Captain John Smith was waiting at the gate. He led her into Jamestown.

"Will you give me the prisoners now?" she asked.

"Let us talk first," he said.

They walked through the town.

"You could have set the prisoners free without me," she said. "Why did you want me here?"

"I wanted to see you," he answered. "I wanted you to talk to your father for me."

"What shall I say?" she asked.

"Tell him I do not want war with him," said John Smith. "Tell him his men must not come here and try to carry off our guns and the tools we use. We took your men prisoner and we beat them. We did it to teach them a lesson. Will you tell your father this?"

"Yes," she said.

They stopped on the pier that had been built out over the river. He said, "You are very quiet. I think you are angry with me. Pocahontas, you must not be angry—or sad. Some day this trouble will be forgotten."

"Do you think so?" she asked.

"Yes, yes," he said. "Some day we will all be friends."

"And you have not forgotten your promise?"

"What promise?" he asked.

"To take me with you when you go to England."

"No, I have not forgotten," he said. "How the people will look when we go driving through London! We will dress you in all your beads and feathers. I will say, 'Here she is—the Indian princess! Here is the beautiful Pocahontas from far-off Virginia!' "

"I do not want the people to look at me," she said.

"They *will* look at you. There will be no way to stop them," he said. "Never fear. I'll be there. I'll not let them come too near."

He was laughing. She began to laugh, too. "When will it be?" she asked.

"I have no way of knowing. I am needed here now," he said.

"But when you go, you will take me with you?"

"Yes, Pocahontas," he said. "We shall go together."

They went back through the town. He showed her a small house made of logs. There were bars at the windows and door.

"Your father's men are here," he told her.

He opened the door. The two men came out. They looked angry and ashamed.

"Tell them they may go," John Smith told Pocahontas. "Tell them never to come back unless they come as friends."

He was not laughing now. His mouth was set. His eyes were cold. Pocahontas felt that he had become a stranger to her.

Then, suddenly, he smiled. "You, Pocahontas, are always welcome. Come to us often."

She went away with the two men. They went down the river bank to where Comochok and Rawhunt were waiting.

It was night when they reached home. The guards at the gate let them into the dark village.

Powhatan sent the men away and sat with Pocahontas outside the house.

"Were you in the palefaces' village?" he asked.

"Yes," she said.

"Are they ready for war?"

"They do not want war," she said. "Captain John Smith told me."

"You believed him?"

"I believed him, yes."

"What are they doing—these men of Jamestown?" he asked.

"I did not see many," she said. "Some may have gone to look for gold. Captain John Smith tells them they must work, but many will not listen. And there is much work to be done. Their houses are not all finished. They do not keep the weeds out of their fields. Father, if I could take the children to Jamestown, we could hoe the fields in only a day or two."

"These are the people who beat our men and put them in prison," he said, "and you would hoe their fields so they can have more food. When they are strong from eating the food, they will drive us out of our homes."

"They do not want to drive us out," she said.

"Do you know more than I?" he said.

"No," she answered.

"Then be quiet," he said. "Be quiet and go to bed!"

13

The summer was warm. Pocahontas grew weary of the long, lazy days. She was lonely, and Captain John Smith was far away. He had gone down the river to the Bay of Chesapeake to make a map of the country for his king.

In the early fall Tom Savage went to Jamestown. For three days he visited his people. He brought back news. Captain John Smith had returned from the Bay of Chesapeake. Captain Newport had come from England, and Namontack had come back with him.

Powhatan was pleased. "We can trade with Captain Newport. He gives us what we ask for."

Captain Newport and a party of men came to the village. Namontack was with them.

Shouts went up. "Our brother has come home!" "Namontack has come from the land across the sea!"

Pocahontas heard the shouts. She saw the young man dressed in the clothes of an Englishman.

But Namontack was forgotten when she saw that Captain John Smith was in the party.

She caught both his hands. She led him away from the others.

They sat under the beech tree. He told her of his voyage on the Bay of Chesapeake and the strange Indian tribes he had met.

"It was a fine adventure. I was sorry to end it," he said, "but now we must make ready for winter."

"Did your fields bear good crops?" she asked.

"No. Our men are not farmers," he said. "Captain Newport brought food from England, enough to last a while." He told her, "Captain Newport brought something more."

"What?" she asked.

"Gifts," he said. "Gifts to your father from the king of England. You will see them tomorrow."

The next day the Englishmen were still there. They met the wide, flat boat that had sailed up the river from Jamestown.

"The gifts are here," John Smith told Pocahontas.

On the boat was something that looked like a wooden box with a tall pole at each corner.

"What is it?" she asked.

"A bed," he said, "and there are more gifts just as fine."

Powhatan sat on a throne in the middle of the village. Englishmen carried the gifts to him. Besides the bed, there were a large copper jug and bowl, a red robe, and a crown.

"The king of England wears such a crown on his head," said Captain Newport. "It is right that King Powhatan should have one, as well. Kneel, so that I may place it on your head."

Powhatan was not listening. He had come down from his throne and was putting on the red robe.

Namontack told Powhatan, "Kneel, and let Captain Newport put the crown on your head."

"Kneel? I kneel to no one," said Powhatan. "I am the king!"

"Good king, I can hardly reach so high," said Captain Newport. He rose on his toes and set the crown on Powhatan's head.

Two of the Englishmen fired their pistols into the air.

Powhatan started forward. The crown slid down over one eye.

"Do not fear," said Captain John Smith. "Guns are fired in England when a king is crowned."

Some of the Englishmen were trying not to laugh. Powhatan gave them a fierce look.

Captain Newport was making a speech. "So we crown you, King Powhatan, and bring you these gifts of friendship."

"I give you thanks," said Powhatan, "and I have gifts for you."

His gifts were an old fur cloak with most of the hair worn off, a pair of his old shoes, and a few baskets of corn.

When the English left, Namontack stayed behind. Pocahontas spoke to him. "Will you not go back to Jamestown with the others?"

"I shall not go back," he said. "I shall never live among the English again."

"Do you not belong to Captain Newport?" she asked.

"No. He showed me to his friends in England. Now he needs me no longer," said Namontack.

"Was he not kind to you?" she asked.

"Kind enough," he said, "but the ways of the English are not our ways." He said in an angry whisper, "You saw them. They laughed at our king. But he turned the joke on them. Did you see their faces when he gave them his old cloak and shoes and a few baskets of corn? They brought gifts only because they wanted more in return. They wanted many furs and many, many baskets of corn."

"You should not say these things," she said. "We must be friends with the Englishmen."

"I speak the truth," he said. "Someday you will know."

14

Another winter had come. The roofs of the village were white with snow. In their wigwams the people were warm, and their storehouses were filled with food.

In Jamestown the English were cold and starving. This was the word brought by Powhatan's spies.

"I must take them food," said Pocahontas.

"You took them food before," said Powhatan, "and now they rise against us. Do you not listen to what our men tell us? Captain John Smith leads his people into our villages. If they do not sell him food, he takes it."

"He takes the food only to keep from starving," she said. "Let us help him. He is your son and my brother."

"He is my son and your brother no longer," said Powhatan. "Do not speak of this again."

A thin young Englishman came to the village. "I come from Captain Smith," he said. "Will you sell us food?"

"You knew winter was coming," said Powhatan. "Why did you not make ready for it?"

"We tried, but our crops were poor," said the Englishman.

"Captain Newport brought food on his ship," said Powhatan. "I heard him say so."

"He and his sailors stayed on for many weeks," said the Englishman. "By the time they sailed for England, they had eaten all the cheese and most of the grain."

Powhatan said to the man, "Take this message to Captain John Smith. It would please me to have a house such as the English have. Tell him to send men to build it for me."

"For this you will give us food?" asked the Englishman.

"I have more to say," said Powhatan. "Tell him I want a stone for making knives sharp. This he promised me long ago. I want fifty long knives and many fire-sticks. I want many beads and pieces of copper. Send me these, and I will load your boat with corn."

The Englishman went away.

A few days later three strange palefaces came to the village. Captain John Smith had sent them, they said. They had come to build an English house for the king.

Powhatan set them to work. His house was to be on a little hill near the village.

The men sang at their work.

"They are happy to be here," Tom Savage said to Pocahontas. "They would like to stay always. They say they never had enough to eat in Jamestown. They say the English were not good to them."

"Are they not English?" she asked.

"No," he said. "They are Dutchmen. They came from their own country to work for the English."

After a few more days the thin young Englishman came back to the village.

"Captain Smith is here," he said. "He has come for the boatload of corn you promised."

Powhatan looked toward the river. "I see no boat," he said.

The Englishman told him what had happened. Their boat was half a mile down the river. It was caught on a sandbar. The men had had to wade ashore.

"We found a house there," he said. "The man and woman in the house took fright when they saw us. They ran away. We were wet and cold, so we went in to warm ourselves. The others are there now. Captain Smith sent me ahead. He asks if you will send him some men."

"Why should I send him men?" asked Powhatan.

"To help lift our boat off the sandbar," said the Englishman, "and to bring us food, as well."

Pocahontas said, "I will take food."

"No," said her father. "This is not the time."

He went with the Englishman. Warriors came out of their houses and followed. The Dutchmen went, too.

Pocahontas stood in the doorway of the king's house. She was sorry they had gone without her, but she was happy that Captain John Smith was near. She would see him soon, she thought. She hoped he would not be thin and hungry-looking.

She pushed the flat stones close to the fire. "I am going to make corn cakes for Captain John Smith," she said to her mother.

Just before dark her father came home. He spoke to Pocahontas' mother. "Call the women and children. We are going to the hiding-place."

Pocahontas stood still. "Is there war?" she asked. But she knew the answer before he spoke.

15

✤✤✤ *THE HIDING-PLACE* ✤✤✤

It was dusk when they left the village. Night came quickly. They walked in a long line, one behind the other. No one spoke. No child cried.

In the darkness Pocahontas could see only a little way before her. She knew her father was ahead, with the four men who guarded him. The three Dutchmen were there, too. All the rest were women and children.

She knew what it meant when the women and children were sent into hiding. It meant that war had begun.

But how had it begun, and why? She asked herself over and over, What has happened?

They walked a long way beside a stream. They pushed through a thicket of pines. Pocahontas felt sand and rocks under her feet. The line came to a stop. They had reached the hiding-place.

Once it had been a village where Powhatan went to hunt in the summer. Now only a few houses were left. They were deep in a tangle of vines and thorn-bushes.

The people crowded into the two largest houses. Pocahontas sat beside her mother. She felt the wind blow in through holes in the wall. "There is snow in the air," she said.

"Good," said her mother. "It will cover our tracks."

Pocahontas slept and woke and slept again. Early in the morning she woke and went to look for her father. She found him in the next wigwam. He was sitting with a deer-skin robe over his head.

"Father," she asked, "where is the fighting?"

"I do not know," he said. "There may be no fighting yet."

"Then why are we here?" she asked.

"There was danger," he said. "Captain John Smith had come for corn."

"Did you not promise him a boatload?" she asked.

"Only if he paid," said Powhatan. "He said he could not pay my price. He said his people were hungry and could not wait. Then I learned what he meant to do. He meant to take me prisoner."

"No!" she said.

"It is true. Our people would have paid a great price to set me free," said Powhatan. "Captain John Smith could have asked for *all* our food."

"How do you know this?" she asked.

"I learned it from my friends, the Dutchmen," he answered. "They have turned against Smith. They told me his plans."

"I do not believe the Dutchmen," she said.

"Do not believe them, then," he said. "Believe Captain John Smith instead!"

She said no more. She went back to her mother.

Late in the day one of her sisters told her that Rawhunt had come from the village.

Pocahontas went at once to look for him. She asked at the next wigwam, "Where is Rawhunt?"

"He and the king went outside," a woman answered.

"Is there fighting in the village? Did Rawhunt say?" asked Pocahontas.

"He did not say," answered the woman.

"I am going to ask him," said Pocahontas.

"They wished to talk *alone*," said the woman. "Wait."

Pocahontas did not wait. She had found the men's tracks in the fresh snow. She followed them. They led to a wigwam that was almost hidden by vines.

She heard voices inside.

"Where are the Englishmen now?" her father was asking.

She stopped to hear the answer.

Rawhunt said, "Some are in the river. They are moving their boat through the ice. The rest stand guard with their firesticks ready. Tomorrow they will have the boat to shore. Then, they say, they will fill it with corn."

"Smith must die," said Powhatan. "They must all die."

"They are always on guard," said Rawhunt, "and how can we fight against their firesticks?"

"Where will they be tonight?" asked Powhatan.

"I think they will sleep again in Wanco's house," said Rawhunt.

"This is what you must do," said Powhatan. "Go tonight and speak to them as if you are friends. Take them food, the best we have. They will gather to eat it. They will put down their firesticks. The warriors must be ready. They must take the Englishmen by surprise."

"Yes!" said Rawhunt.

"Smith must not escape," said Powhatan. "Without their leader, the Englishmen cannot stand against us."

Pocahontas went quietly away.

Some of the women were breaking small branches off a pine tree. "Help us," one of them said. "We are gathering branches for the floor of our wigwam. They will make a soft bed."

Pocahontas helped them.

While they worked, the sky grew darker. Snow and rain began to fall. They carried the branches into the wigwam.

"You are pale, Pocahontas," said her mother. "Sit here and rest."

"I am not tired," said Pocahontas.

A little later she said, "I am going to the next house. I shall stay there tonight with my sisters."

"Do not go into the storm," said her mother.

Pocahontas pretended not to hear. She went out toward the next wigwam, but she did not sleep there. She stepped out of sight among the bushes. She began to run.

16

✛✛✛ *IN THE NIGHT* ✛✛✛

The wind was at her back, and she ran as if she were flying. She ran until night came. Then she could only walk and feel her way among the trees.

Once she fell. She lay with her face in the snow. For a moment she rested.

But there was no time to rest. She got to her feet and went on.

She walked without stopping until she came to the river. She was on the broad, flat path near the village.

"Wanco's house," Rawhunt had said. It was nearby, on the river bank. She turned toward it.

Now the wind was in her face. The rain and snow

blinded her. She put a hand to her eyes and looked out between her fingers. She saw a light.

"Stop!" said a voice.

She tried to run.

Someone caught her arm.

"Who are you?" asked the voice.

Two men were there.

"I must see Captain John Smith," she said.

"Pocahontas!" said one of the men.

"*Are* you Pocahontas?" asked the other.

"Yes," she said.

She went with them. She saw the shape of Wanco's

house ahead. Light came from beneath the mat that hung over the doorway.

Inside the house there was firelight. A band of Englishmen sat about the fire.

One of them was Captain John Smith.

"Pocahontas!" He sprang up off the floor. "Are you alone?"

"Yes," she said.

He spoke to the men who had brought her. "Go back and keep watch."

The two men left. John Smith said to Pocahontas, "Come to the fire. Sit here."

"There is not time," she said. "Listen to what I say. Tonight our men will come to this house. They will bring food and speak as friends. But when you put aside your firesticks and begin to eat, they will try to kill you."

"How do you know this?" asked Captain John Smith.

"I cannot tell you," she said, "but it is true."

She was at the door.

"Wait," he said.

"Let me go,"she said. "If they knew I had come to you, they would kill me."

"First we must thank you." He asked the other men, "What presents shall we give—?"

"No!" she cried. "I want no present. How could I take one? They would see it and know I had come to you."

She lifted the mat that hung over the doorway. She looked at him once more and was gone.

17

It was not yet morning when she reached the hiding-place. Her hands and face were numb with cold. She thought she had never been so weary before.

She put her head into the wigwam where she had left her mother. A few coals burned in the fire-pit. By their light she could see the sleeping women and children. She lay down beside her mother.

"Pocahontas?" said her mother.

"Yes," whispered Pocahontas. "I could not sleep, so I came back."

"Foolish child, to come out into the storm," said her mother. "Your hair is wet."

She went back to sleep, and Pocahontas slept, too.

The next day Rawhunt came again. He and Powhatan talked alone.

Pocahontas tried to guess what they had said. Their faces told her nothing.

After another day Powhatan said, "The danger is past."

He led them through the woods to the village.

Pocahontas found Nantaquas. He had not gone to the hiding-place. He had stayed with the warriors.

"Where are the Englishmen?" she asked.

"Gone," he said.

"Was there a battle?" she asked.

"There was no battle," he answered. "We had a plan. When it was night, we meant to take food to the Englishmen. While they ate, we meant to attack them by surprise. Most of all, we meant to kill Captain John Smith."

"But you did not!" she said.

"No," said Nantaquas. "We took the food. They would not eat. For half the night we waited outside. All the time they stood with their firesticks, ready for battle. They seemed to know our plan. At last we came back to the village."

"Where did they go?" she asked.

"To Jamestown, with their boat full of our corn," he said.

"You gave it to them?" she asked.

"What could we do? They came to the village. Captain John Smith said, 'Do as we ask, or there will be war.' The firesticks were pointed at our heads. We had to do as he asked. We loaded the boat with corn. If you go hungry this winter, blame your brother, Captain John Smith."

"He took the corn because his people were starving," she said. "He will pay for it when he can."

Nantaquas laughed. It was an ugly laugh. "Whatever he did, you would say it was right. But I know who our enemy is, and our father knows. We all know but you."

Pocahontas thought, If they knew what I have done, they would kill me.

She went away before Nantaquas could see that she was afraid.

Near the end of winter a visitor stopped at the village. He was a man of another tribe. He had just come from Jamestown.

Many men there had died of a fever, he said, but more had come from England to take their places. Captain John Smith and his little army were going up and down the land. Sometimes they went to trade, sometimes to fight.

The English seemed to be everywhere. They were in the woods. They were on the river.

Powhatan said, "We are leaving this place. We shall move to Oropax."

Oropax was his village deep in the woods. It was a day's walk to the north.

"You have your English house here," said Pocahontas. "Will you leave it so soon?"

The Dutchmen had finished Powhatan's house. It was made of wood, with a door that opened and closed. It had windows, a floor, and a fireplace.

Powhatan was proud of his house. He showed it to his friends. Every day he made a fire in the fireplace. He liked to stand outside and see the smoke come out of the chimney.

"Some day we may come back," he said, "but now I

am tired of living in this place."

There was another reason, she thought. He was leaving because the English had come too close.

They moved to Oropax. The women carried loads of mats and tools and clothing. They marked out new fields and planted crops.

Oropax was set on high ground. All about it were oaks and maples and small flowering trees.

"Is it not better here?" asked Powhatan. "This was always a pleasant spot."

"Yes, it is pleasant," said Pocahontas. Still, she missed the old village. She missed the beech tree and the river, and she was far from Jamestown now.

She asked Hapsis, "Do you think Captain John

Smith knows where I have gone?"

"I think so," answered the old woman.

"He may come looking for me," said Pocahontas.

"Yes, he may," said Hapsis.

"If he goes to England, he is sure to come here first," said Pocahontas. "He would not go without me."

All that summer she waited for a message from Captain John Smith.

In the fall Tom Savage went to Jamestown.

Powhatan had said, "It is long since you have seen your people. Go to them. Visit for a day."

Pocahontas knew why he wished Tom to go. He wanted news of Smith and his army.

She, too, wished Tom to go. She was sure he would bring her a message from Captain John Smith.

When Tom Savage came back, he went first to her father's house. Pocahontas sat a little way from the wigwam. She waited for him to come out. While she waited, she sang to herself.

Tom came outside. He looked strange, almost as if he had been crying.

"Is my father angry?" she asked.

He shook his head.

"What is wrong?" she asked.

"Pocahontas," he said, "I went to Jamestown——"

"I know that," she said. "Did you see Captain John Smith?"

"I did see him," answered Tom.

"What did he say?" she asked.

"Pocahontas—" said Tom. "Pocahontas, he is dead!" She sat still.

"I saw him on the ship," said Tom, "just before it sailed, and—"

She asked in a whisper, "How did he die?"

"He and his men were in a boat," said Tom. "They had gunpowder, and it caught fire. It burned him. It burned a great hole in his side. He wanted to die in England. His men put him on the ship, and it sailed with him. I saw the look on his face, and I could tell— I could tell—"

She got up and began to walk away. She walked until she was alone among the trees. She stood there for a while. Once she spoke Captain John Smith's name. She did not speak again for many days.

Part Two

18

∔∔∔ *THE ENGLISH SHIP* ∔∔∔

The young people had been swimming. Now they rested and dried themselves in the sun. Behind them was the village. Before them were the shining waters of the Potomac River.

Most of the young people were Pocahontas' cousins. All were her friends.

She said, "I wish I could stay with you always."

"Then stay," said one of the men.

"I cannot," she said. "Think how long I have been here already. I came in the time of snows. Now it is near the time of blossoms."

"A visit should be as long as you like," said a girl cousin.

"No, I must go soon," said Pocahontas, "or my father will send someone after me."

"We will hide you," said the cousin. "We will say you went to England in a great canoe."

Some of the others laughed. Pocahontas did not laugh. She was remembering a promise once made to her. Captain John Smith had promised that they would someday go to England together. She was remembering Captain John Smith.

It was three years since he had left her. She never spoke his name now, but she thought of him. She could not think of him without feeling sad.

Japazaws and his wife came down to the shore. It was in their wigwam that Pocahontas was staying.

Japazaws was a short man with a long, thin face. Tassana, his wife, was plump and pretty. They had been running and were out of breath.

"There is an English ship—around the bend!" said Japazaws.

The ship came into sight.

"Make it stop!" said Tassana, like a child.

He stood at the edge of the water. He waved both hands. The ship began to swing toward shore.

Men and women came out of the village. A few had furs and baskets. They were ready to trade with the Englishmen.

The Englishmen, too, were ready to trade. Some of them came ashore with strings of beads on their arms. Others had pans and kettles and cloth.

"I am Captain Argall," said the leader. "Show us what you have to trade."

"We have what you see here," said Japazaws.

"No more than this?" said Captain Argall. Pocahontas saw that he and his men were disappointed.

She started away. She did not like the captain. His smile was mocking, and his eyes were too bold.

Tassana called to her. "Do not go, Pocahontas. Come and see this copper kettle."

"'Pocahontas,' did you say?" Captain Argall asked quickly. "Is she the king's daughter?"

"Yes," said Japazaws.

"I wish to speak with her," said Captain Argall. "Ask her to stop."

Pocahontas did not stop. She went on into the woods. There she stayed until evening. By that time, she thought, the Englishmen would be gone.

But when she went back to Japazaws' wigwam, Captain Argall was there.

He made a low bow. "I am happy to see you again, princess," he said.

She felt that he was laughing at her.

"May I not call you 'princess'?" he asked. "It is our name for the daughter of a king."

"I know the name," she said.

"Sit and talk with us," said Japazaws. "The captain has something to ask you."

"I hear that you are soon going home," said Captain Argall. "May I take you there on my ship?"

"I do not wish to go on the ship," said Pocahontas.

She went outside. She did not go back to Japazaws' wigwam that night. She slept in the house of a girl cousin.

In the morning Tassana scolded her. "Captain Argall is our friend, yet you did not make him welcome. Why are you angry with him?"

"I am not angry," said Pocahontas.

"He thinks you are," said Tassana.

"I do not like the way he speaks. I do not like the look in his eyes," said Pocahontas, "but I am not angry."

"Then will you go to the ship with us?" asked Tassana. "Will you say good-by to him?"

"If it will make you happy," said Pocahontas, "I will say good-by."

She went with Tassana and Japazaws. The Englishmen were ready to sail. The little bridge had been put down from the ship to the shore.

Captain Argall was on deck. "Come aboard," he said to Tassana and Japazaws. "Let me show you the ship."

"I want to see." Tassana caught Pocahontas' hand.

"I have seen English ships before," said Pocahontas. "Go without me, you and Japazaws."

"It would not be right," said Tassana. "I would be the only woman on the ship, and I would feel strange."

"Come with us, Pocahontas," said Japazaws. "If you do not, Captain Argall will think you are not friendly. He may not stop to trade here again."

Tassana was pulling at her arm. Pocahontas went with her and Japazaws over the little bridge.

Captain Argall showed them about the ship.

"Will you change your mind, Pocahontas?" he asked. "Will you let me take you to your father?"

"No," she said.

Tassana saw the stairway. "Where does it go?" she asked, and she went below.

She began to call to Pocahontas, "Come! Here is something you must see!"

Pocahontas followed her.

"How can you see anything?" she said. "It is so dark—"

Tassana gave an odd little laugh. She ran past Pocahontas and back up the stairs.

Pocahontas said to herself, Foolish woman—always playing a game.

She started up the stairs and met Captain Argall on his way down.

"Pocahontas—" he said.

She tried to move past him. He caught both her hands. He was quick and strong.

"Let me go!" She began to fight. "Japazaws! Tassana!"

"They will not help you," he said. "They are on shore."

Another man came down the stairs. He put his hand over her mouth.

She heard the voices of the people on shore. They were calling good-by to the Englishmen as the ship pulled away.

19

Pocahontas lay in the bottom of the ship. Her hands were tied.

One of the men came down and lifted her to her feet. He helped her up the stairs. Captain Argall was waiting on deck.

She held out her hands. "Take off this rope," she said.

"So you can jump into the water and swim off like a fish?" said Captain Argall. "No, princess."

"You have tricked me—you and Japazaws and his wife," she said. "Did you pay them well? Did you give her the copper kettle she wanted?"

He only smiled.

She asked, "Why have you done this?"

"We need your help," he said.

"You think I would ever help you?"

"Yes, I think so." He told her, "We are going to keep you with us for a while. We are going to keep you until your father does as we ask."

"What do you want from him?" she asked.

"He has English prisoners," said Captain Argall. "He has guns that were stolen from us. When he gives back our men and guns, we will let you go."

They landed at Jamestown. Men were on the pier to meet the ship. And there were women!

They looked strange in their dresses that hid their arms and hung to the ground!

In the three years Pocahontas had been away, the town had changed. There were many more houses. Smoke from the chimneys hung on the air like fog. Among all the faces turned up toward her, she saw none that she knew.

Captain Argall asked her, "If we untie you, do you promise not to run?"

"I do not promise," she said.

She went with him off the ship and through the town. A crowd of people followed. "Who is she?" they asked. "What has she done?"

They came to a house of logs and stone.

Captain Argall led her inside. He untied her hands. He pushed her into a room and shut the door after her.

She looked about the damp, dirty room. There was a wooden bench in a corner. There was a window with bars across it.

She tried the door. It was locked. She sat down and rubbed her hands where the rope had left red marks.

A spider was spinning its web across the window. She watched it until the room began to grow dark.

The door opened and a man came in. He wore a long, black coat. He spoke, and his voice was kind. "Are you truly Pocahontas, daughter of Powhatan?"

"Yes, truly," she answered.

"I am the governor of Jamestown," he said. "I have talked with Captain Argall. You may say it was wrong of him to bring you here—"

"I do say it," she said.

"But it was wrong of your father to make prisoners

of our men. It is wrong of him to keep the guns that were stolen from us. Until he sends back our men and guns, you shall stay with us. Do you understand me, child?"

"I am no child," she said.

"You are no older than my daughters," he said. "I cannot leave you in this place. Come."

They left the prison. She walked beside him.

They came to a new house near the river.

"This is my home," he said.

Two girls were in the doorway.

"These are my daughters," he said, "Mary and Betsy."

The girl called Mary had long, dark hair. Betsy had yellow curls such as Pocahontas had never seen before. Both girls were excited, and their eyes were bright.

"They told me I should bring you here," said the governor. "Come in, Pocahontas."

"Pocahontas—is that your name?" asked Betsy.

"Yes," said Pocahontas.

"Are you really a princess?" asked Mary.

"My father is the king," said Pocahontas.

"Then she *is* a princess!" said Mary to her sister.

"Will you stay with us?" asked Betsy.

"With you?" said Pocahontas. "Am I not a prisoner?"

"We need not keep you under lock and key," said the governor. "You are free to come and go in Jamestown. You must not leave the town. Do you understand?"

"I understand," she said.

"You cannot run away if you try," he told her. "Our guards are along the river and the wall."

She thought, Your talk of guards does not frighten me. You cannot keep me here.

20

The next morning Governor Gates went out into Jamestown. The three girls were left alone.

Mary and Betsy took Pocahontas through the house. She saw the rugs and the oak chairs and tables. She saw the blue dishes and silver candlesticks.

The girls showed Pocahontas their dresses.

Mary took a black dress out of a chest. "This was our mother's," she said. "She never wore it. She died on the ship on the way to Virginia."

Pocahontas touched the dress. She touched the others spread out on the bed. "So many," she said.

"Oh, these are only a few," said Betsy. "In England I had twenty dresses. We don't need so many here."

"Do you want to dress up, Pocahontas?" asked Mary. "Here—try this."

She helped Pocahontas into a dress. It was of plum-colored linen with black braid down the front.

Pocahontas walked across the room. She liked the feel of the cloth. But who could run in such a dress? Who could climb a tree?

"Something is wrong," said Betsy.

"Her hair," said Mary.

They combed Pocahontas' hair. They braided it and tied it with a ribbon.

They brought shoes and stockings. Pocahontas put them on. They fit very well.

"You look like an English lady," said Mary.

"Let's take her out walking," said Betsy, "so everyone can see her."

They walked about Jamestown. People talked with them on the street.

A woman called to them from her doorway.

"She is Mistress Morris," said Mary. "She helps our father look after us."

The girls stopped to visit Mistress Morris. She gave them tea in china cups.

Back at the governor's house, Betsy brought in wood for the fireplace. Mary made fried-cakes.

"Shall I help?" asked Pocahontas.

"You are a princess," said Betsy.

"In my tribe there are many princesses," said Pocahontas. "There is none who does not work."

So they set her to sweeping and dusting.

The three of them cooked supper. It was ready when Governor Gates came home.

While they sat at supper, Pocahontas heard the sound of a bell. She lifted her head to listen. The sound was deep and clear. It was like music.

"What is it?" she asked.

"The church bell," said Mary.

"Why does it ring?" asked Pocahontas.

"To tell us it is time for church," said Mary.

They all went to church. It was a fine, new building. There were benches of cedar. There were large, pointed windows.

The church was filled with people. A man in black stood before them. He spoke for a long time.

Afterward Pocahontas asked the Gates girls, "What was he saying? What did he mean?"

"He was preaching," said Mary. "He was saying that God loves us and we must love God."

"He was saying that we must try to do what God wishes us to do," said Betsy.

"How do you know what God wishes you to do?" asked Pocahontas.

"It is all here in the Bible." Betsy brought her a thick, black book.

Pocahontas looked inside it. "I wish I could read these words."

"We can teach you," said Mary.

"No," said Pocahontas. "There will not be time."

The Gates girls had a bedroom of their own. They made a bed for Pocahontas next to theirs.

They went to bed early. Pocahontas lay awake in the dark. When she thought Mary and Betsy were asleep, she got up. Very quietly she put on her deerskin dress and moccasins. She felt her way to the front door. She went outside.

The moon was up. The night was almost as bright as day. Surely there was no way to walk through the streets without being seen.

Somewhere in the town a dog began to bark. A light came on in a window.

This was not the time to run away. Pocahontas went back into the house.

The next day she thought the time had come.

She and the Gates family were at supper. Mistress Morris came through the yard and called, as she ran past, "Master Hood's house is on fire!"

The governor dropped his spoon and ran after her. Mary and Betsy followed him.

Pocahontas was left alone.

She stood on the doorstep. People were running down the street. No one looked at her.

She went quickly toward the wall. The gate was open, and she started through.

A voice said, "Go back."

There was a man outside the wall with a firestick in his hands. He was young and tall. He had heavy, black brows, and his face was stern.

"You are not to go outside the town," he said.

"Not even into the woods?" she asked.

"No," he said.

"You think I would run away?" she asked.

"I think you might try," he answered.

"Would you shoot me?" she asked.

He looked as if he did not know what to say.

"Would you?" she asked.

"Perhaps not," he said, "but there are others who would."

Mary and Betsy came to the gate. They were calling her name.

"There she is," said Betsy.

"We couldn't find you," said Mary. "We didn't know where you had gone."

"Master Hood's roof was burning, but it was only a small fire," said Betsy. "It was out before we got there."

"Come, Pocahontas," said Mary. "Father says we must finish our supper."

Pocahontas asked, on the way to the house, "Who was the man at the gate?"

"That was John Rolfe," Betsy told her.

"Master Rolfe is a good man," said Mary. "Father wishes we had more like him in Jamestown."

They talked about John Rolfe as they had the rest of their supper.

"On his way to Virginia his ship was wrecked in the Bermudas," said Mary.

Betsy told Pocahontas, "The Bermudas are islands a long way out in the sea."

"He and the rest of the people lived there for months," said Mary. "They built two small ships out of the one that was wrecked, and they sailed to Jamestown in the two ships. Master Rolfe's wife and baby were with him. They named the baby Bermuda because she was born there."

"His wife and the baby died," said Betsy. "They say he wanted to die, too. But that was two years ago. Now he laughs sometimes, and he plays games with the other men."

The church bells were ringing.

"Clear the table," said the governor. "It is half an hour until prayer meeting."

"Do you go to church every night?" asked Pocahontas.

"Every night," said Mary.

"And twice on Sunday," said Betsy.

Pocahontas went to prayer meeting with the Gates family. Just inside the church she saw John Rolfe. He did not speak, but he looked at her as she went by.

21

✦✦✦ *THE THREE CANOES* ✦✦✦

Captain Argall had sent a man to Powhatan with a message: "Give us the Englishmen you hold as slaves. Give us the guns and tools you took from us. Give us four canoes full of corn. Then shall Pocahontas be returned to you."

In three days the man was back with Powhatan's answer: "I shall do as you ask."

Governor Gates brought the news to Pocahontas.

They waited. Days went by.

"Why does my father not send for me?" Pocahontas said to the Gates girls.

"Why do you want to leave us?" asked Mary.

"I like being here with you," said Pocahontas, "but I do not like to think I am a prisoner."

"We never think of you as a prisoner," said Mary. "You are the best friend we have."

"It may be that I shall be here always," said Pocahontas. "It may be that my father has forgotten me."

On a day in summer three canoes came down the river. When they pulled up to the pier, a crowd was waiting. Captain Argall was there. Pocahontas was there with the Gates girls.

In the first canoe were the seven Englishmen who had been Powhatan's prisoners. In the second were a few guns and tools. The third canoe was filled with corn.

Comochok was in one of the canoes. "We have come for Pocahontas," he said.

"You have set our men free, it is true," said Captain Argall, "but these are not all the guns and tools you took from us. One canoe full of corn is not enough. Send us three more. Send us the rest of the guns and tools. Then you may take Pocahontas away."

Pocahontas asked Comochok, "What word did my father send me?"

"No word," answered Comochok.

"Why did he not send all the tools and firesticks?" she asked. "Why did he not send four canoes full of corn? Am I not worth more to him than these things?"

"We have done what we could," said Comochok.

Pocahontas went away. She sat down in the shade of the wall. Perhaps she would never go home again, she thought. What was there for her at home? Her mother and Hapsis had died. Nantaquas had married and gone to another village. Tom Savage had long ago gone back to England. And her father had changed. Now he cared more for his corn and a few tools and firesticks than for her.

The Gates girls came looking for her.

"We could not find you," said Mary. "We were afraid you had run away."

"Do not be afraid," said Pocahontas. "I shall not run away."

She tried to be happy in Jamestown.

The Gates girls taught her to read a little. She

learned the names of the days and the months. She learned that each year had a number, and that this year was 1612.

Mistress Morris helped her make two dresses and an apron.

The young minister, Richard Buck, read to her from the Bible.

Sometimes she and John Rolfe worked side by side in the fields.

Summer rain came to Jamestown. The roofs leaked. The streets turned to mud. People became ill from living in their damp houses.

Pocahontas came home from Mistress Morris' one day and found Mary and Betsy crying.

"Father is going to send us away!" said Mary. "He says we must sail for England on the next ship."

"He thinks we will be ill if we stay here," said Betsy.

"Besides, he thinks we should be in school," said Mary.

"How can we leave our father and our friends?" cried Betsy. "How can we leave you, Pocahontas?"

For days they wept and begged their father to let

them stay. But when the next ship sailed, they were on board. With tears running down their cheeks, they stood on deck and waved good-by.

Pocahontas went to live in Mistress Morris' house. She helped with the cooking and housecleaning. Every day she and Mistress Morris went to church together.

The minister came often to the house. He said to Pocahontas, "You must have a name from the Bible. Shall we call you Mary or Elizabeth or Ruth or Rebecca?"

She said the names over to herself. The one she liked best was Rebecca. She told Mistress Morris, "My name is Pocahontas Rebecca."

John Rolfe came to the house almost as often as the minister. He read to Pocahontas and Mistress Morris from a book of poems. Pocahontas did not understand much of the poems, but the sound of his voice pleased her.

Christmas came. All day the church was crowded. That night John Rolfe came to call on Pocahontas.

"At Christmas time we give gifts," he said, "and I have one for you."

His gift was a wooden chain.

"I made it myself," he said.

She wore it around her neck.

She had copper earrings. She had necklaces of beads and shells. But she liked the wooden chain best of all.

22

Governor Gates was lonely without his daughters. Before many weeks he followed them back to England.

Thomas Dale became governor in his place. He was a stern man, with a way of looking at people that made them afraid.

He stopped John Rolfe and Pocahontas on the street one day. "Why does this Indian girl stay here?" he asked. "It is time she was worth something to us."

"She is worth much to us," said John Rolfe. "She helps Mistress Morris and she works in the fields."

"She would be worth more if her father paid the rest of her ransom," said Governor Dale.

"We are waiting for him to pay," said John Rolfe.

"We have waited long enough," said the governor. "It is time we took the girl to her father to see what he will give us for her."

A day passed, and another. Pocahontas thought he had forgotten.

But on the third day he came to Mistress Morris' and said to Pocahontas, "You will come with me."

"Where?" asked Pocahontas.

"To your father's village," said the governor.

"This is her home now," said Mistress Morris. "Please let her stay."

"Be quick," said the governor to Pocahontas.

"May I speak first with my friends?" she asked.

"There is not time," he answered.

She touched Mistress Morris' hand and went with Governor Dale.

The ship was ready to sail. Argall was captain. It was the same ship that had brought her to Jamestown almost a year ago.

She looked at the people on the pier. She had hoped

John Rolfe would come to say good-by, but he was not there.

She went on board. She stood on deck, and the wind blew her long skirt against the rail. What would her people say, she wondered, when they saw her in English clothes?

A man came running toward the ship. He ran across the pier and came on board.

"Pocahontas—!" he said.

It was John Rolfe.

She put out her hand. "Now I can say good-by."

"No," he said. "I am going with you."

They sailed up the river. On board there was an Indian guide named Otchek. Governor Dale had brought him to carry messages to Powhatan.

Pocahontas saw the village ahead. She saw the wall and the beech tree and the house the Dutchmen had made for her father.

John Rolfe stood beside her. "Where are your people?" he asked. "I see no one on shore."

Something struck the water in front of them. It was an arrow.

Someone shouted, "They are shooting at us from behind the trees!"

Captain Argall swung the ship away from shore.

They sailed beyond the village. They anchored in the mouth of a creek.

The governor told Otchek, "Go to Powhatan. Tell him his daughter is on the ship. Ask him what he will give us for her."

Otchek went ashore. They saw him go off through the trees.

Soon he was back. "Powhatan does not believe Pocahontas is here," he said. "He says it is a trick. He says the English only want to come into the village and rob his people."

"Go back to Powhatan," said Governor Dale. "Tell him to send someone to the ship, someone who may see Pocahontas and talk with her. Then he will know it is no trick."

Again Otchek was put ashore.

This time he did not come back until morning. With him were two painted young men from the village.

"My brothers!" cried Pocahontas.

She was happy to see them.

"Is our father well?" she asked.

"He grows old, but he is strong," said one of the brothers. "Are you well, Pocahontas?"

"Yes," she answered. "The English treat me kindly."

"You have changed," said the other brother.

"I am the same," she said. "Only in these clothes I seem different."

"No," he said. "You have changed."

The two men gave Governor Dale a message from Powhatan. He could not pay the rest of the ransom for Pocahontas. Perhaps he could pay some day, but not now.

Pocahontas said to John Rolfe, "No one wants me."

"I want you," he said.

She looked at him quickly.

"If you had gone back to your village," he said, "I meant to come after you. Pocahontas, do you know what I am saying?"

She shook her head.

"I want you to marry me," he said.

23

✦✦✦ *LITTLE NANTAQUAS* ✦✦✦

All Jamestown talked of the wedding.

Mistress Morris made the dress that Pocahontas was to wear. It was of cream-colored linen with white ribbons and lace.

Powhatan was asked to the wedding, but he did not come. Instead he sent an uncle of Pocahontas' and two of her brothers.

The wedding day was a holiday in Jamestown. The church was filled with people.

John Rolfe and the minister waited at the altar. Pocahontas came into the church. She carried a bouquet of spring flowers. Her uncle was beside her. Her two brothers walked behind.

The minister read the wedding service. Pocahontas and John Rolfe knelt before him. John Rolfe had had a ring made from a gold coin. He put it on her finger, and they were man and wife.

Pocahontas' uncle spoke. "Your people and my people—now we shall be at peace."

John Rolfe and Pocahontas did not stay in Jamestown. They went up the river to the new English town of Henrico.

"The land is better here," he said.

He built a house. He planted fruit trees from England. He sowed corn, wheat, oats, and barley. On his farm he planted another crop, which none of the Englishmen had tried to grow before. He planted a field of tobacco.

The tobacco seeds were like golden-brown dust. At first the plants were tiny, but in a little while some had grown as high as his head.

In the fall Pocahontas helped him strip off the leaves.

When the next ship sailed for England, two barrels of John Rolfe's tobacco leaves were on board.

Near the end of the year the ship came back. The captain told John Rolfe, "Your crop brought a high price in London. Plant more tobacco next year. I can sell all you raise."

John Rolfe plowed a larger field for his new crop. He said to his neighbors, "Grow tobacco. It is wanted in London."

In the spring a son was born to Pocahontas and John Rolfe. His father named him Thomas.

"He must have an English name," he said. "He looks more English than Indian."

The baby's skin was fair. His mouth and nose were like his father's. Yet Pocahontas felt that his eyes were like those of her brother Nantaquas.

"Little Nantaquas," she called him when his father was not there.

Before he was a year old the baby could walk and talk. A dozen times a day John Rolfe came in from the fields to be near his son.

Governor Dale came to see the baby.

"Have Pocahontas' people seen him yet?" he asked.

"Some of them," said John Rolfe.

"And Powhatan—has he been here?" asked the governor.

"No," said John Rolfe. "I think he will never come to us."

"Will you go to him?" asked the governor.

"My wife wishes him to see our son," said John Rolfe, "but I do not wish it. Powhatan might try to keep her and the baby there."

"That is true," said Governor Dale. "We have had peace since you were married. We should not risk another war."

Pocahontas was listening. She was sitting in her corner with the baby in her arms.

"Captain Argall and I are sailing soon for England," said the governor. "We are looking for Indians who might sail with us."

"You mean to take Indians to England?" asked John Rolfe.

"Yes. I have friends at home who have never seen an Indian," said Governor Dale. "Our king and queen have never seen one. There are teachers and writers who want to study Indians and ask them questions."

"My wife will go," said John Rolfe.

"No!" she said.

He looked surprised. "There was a time when you wanted to."

"That was long ago," she said. "Now I have you and our son."

"You would have us in England as well as here," he said.

"Would you be with me?" she asked.

"Did you think I would let you go alone? Pocahontas, I have dreamed of taking you and Thomas to England. I want my mother and brothers to see you and our son."

She said, "If you would be there—"

"She will go," John Rolfe said to the governor. "Help me find someone to tend my farm, and we will all go."

"Good," said Governor Dale. "Do you know of other Indians who would sail with us?"

"My sister Mattachanna will be here tomorrow," said Pocahontas. "She may know of someone. She may wish to go with me."

Mattachanna was there the next day with her husband, Tomocomo. She was a smiling, round-faced girl a little younger than Pocahontas. Tomocomo was a strong young man who wore bright colors and many beads.

Pocahontas told them of the governor's plan.

"We will go," said Mattachanna.

"We know of others who might go," said Tomocomo.

So it was that Mattachanna, Tomocomo, and eight

of their friends were on Captain Argall's ship with John Rolfe, Pocahontas, and Baby Thomas. Governor Dale and a few other Englishmen sailed with them.

As the ship was leaving Jamestown, Pocahontas took the baby and went below. Once she would have been happy at the thought of the voyage before her. Now she felt strange, as if she were waiting to wake from a dream.

24

The voyage was long. Pocahontas grew weary of the gray waters and stormy skies. The other Indians were weary, too.

One day a sailor tried to show them land ahead.

"No, no," they said. "It is only more water. We shall never see land again." But soon they were sailing along the coast of England.

At the sight of trees and fields, the Indians were happy and excited. They looked in wonder at the cities and towns.

The ship sailed up the River Thames to the city of London.

John Rolfe showed Pocahontas the Tower of London.

Captain John Smith had once told her of the Tower. She looked up at the high, gray walls. "So tall!" she said.

"And there is London Bridge," said John Rolfe.

She gazed at the great bridge. "How can it be? How could they build it all the way across the river?"

She saw horses pulling carriages and wagons, and she laughed aloud. "How pretty they are, the horses!" she said. "I want one for my own."

They went to an inn in London. The other Indians went with Governor Dale.

Pocahontas liked the room in the inn. She and the

baby could sit by the window and look into the street below. All day people went by. Some were in carriages, some were on foot. Some wore fine clothing. Others wore rags.

"There are many rich, but there are more poor," she said. "Why is that?"

"It has always been so," said John Rolfe.

He had friends in London. He brought them to see his wife and son.

"This is my wife, Rebecca," he would say. Now that they were in England, he hardly ever called her Pocahontas.

People stared at her. They often laughed when she talked. They whispered behind her back.

She was glad when they left London.

They went to the old Rolfe home in the east of England. John Rolfe's mother lived there. His two brothers and their wives were there, too.

Every day the men were gone together. They rode horseback across the fields and along the seashore nearby.

Pocahontas and Thomas were left with the Rolfe women. The women played with Thomas and made clothes for him.

They tried to be kind to Pocahontas, but she felt shy with them. She never knew what to say. Most of the time they talked with one another in their soft, light voices.

Summer passed, and part of fall.

John Rolfe said, "There are others waiting to see us."

They went back to the inn in London. Many people came to the little rooms. Some were lords and ladies.

"You must smile, Rebecca," John Rolfe told her. "When our friends are here, you must look as if you are happy."

She watched the English ladies. She tried to talk and laugh as they did.

But often she was sad. It was because of the weather, she thought. Day after day there was rain.

One afternoon John Rolfe took Thomas to a dog-and-pony show. Pocahontas was left alone.

She grew tired of the little rooms. She wanted to breathe fresh air. She put on a cloak and went down into the street.

Someone called out, "The Indian!" A crowd began to follow her.

She tried to run. Her feet slipped on the wet cobblestones.

Hands reached out. Children were asking for money. "Indian!" they said. "Give us a penny, Indian!"

"I have nothing," she said.

The people came closer. They made a circle around her.

"Let me go!" she cried.

She broke through the crowd. She ran back into the inn and up the stairs.

In her bedroom she fell across the bed. She was coughing and shivering. She pulled the bedclothes about her.

John Rolfe and Thomas came home. Their cheeks were red from the cold. "Horse!" shouted Thomas.

"Yes, we saw a horse," said his father. "What else did we see?"

"Horse!" shouted Thomas again.

"He forgot the dogs. All he remembers are the horses." John Rolfe was looking at Pocahontas. "Is something wrong?"

"No," she answered. "I am resting."

"You should be dressed," he said. "In an hour we go to the theater."

"The theater?" she said.

"Have you forgotten?" he said. "The nurse is coming to look after Thomas while we go out."

Thomas was on his hands and knees.

"Look at him, Rebecca. Our son thinks he is a horse," said John Rolfe. He was laughing. Pocahontas tried to laugh, too, as she got slowly out of bed.

25

Pocahontas went to the theaters. She went to balls and learned the English dances.

She was asked to come to the palace to meet King James and Queen Anne.

A coach and four silver-gray horses came for her and waited outside the inn. Pocahontas was dressed in yellow satin and she carried a fan. John Rolfe went down to the coach with her.

"I wish you might go, too," she said.

"It is you they want to see," he said. "Remember, you are a princess. You belong among kings and queens."

When she came home, he asked her, "What happened? Tell me everything."

"The palace is beautiful," she said. "The king and queen were kind. The queen is a large woman."

"What did you talk about?" he asked.

"About my home," she said.

"What else?" he asked.

"I cannot remember," she said. "I have heard so much and seen so much—it is hard to remember." She looked out into the street. Rain was falling. She said, "Take me away from here."

"Rebecca, we cannot go now," he said. "All London wants to see you. And soon a man will be here to paint your picture."

"Why am I so tired?" she asked. "Once I could work all day and never be tired."

"You must rest more," he said. "Try to sleep late in the morning. After the Christmas holidays we will go away for a while."

All through the holidays they visited with friends. Pocahontas went again to the palace. She had tea with Queen Anne.

On New Year's Day she asked John Rolfe, "What does it mean—New Year's?"

"It means a new year is beginning," John Rolfe told her. "The old year was 1616. The new year is 1617."

"Are the holidays over?" she asked.

"After today they will be over," he said.

"Then let us go away, as you promised," she said.

But Mattachanna and Tomocomo stopped on their way through the city. They were going to live with an English family. They liked being in England, they said, although some of the other Indians wanted to go home.

After they had gone, John Rolfe's mother came for a visit.

It was weeks before Pocahontas and Thomas and John Rolfe could leave London.

They went to a village just outside the city. There they had rooms in an inn.

The village was small and quiet. Pocahontas felt that London, with its smoke and noise, was far away.

On a chill winter morning she and John Rolfe were

having tea. Thomas was playing with a toy wagon.

Pocahontas heard a carriage stop at the front door. A man's voice came to her. Long ago she had heard such a voice.

She put down her cup. Her hand was shaking.

Someone was climbing the stairs. Someone knocked. John Rolfe opened the door.

Pocahontas saw the man outside. He was older now. His hair was more gray than gold. But even before he spoke his name, she knew him.

"Good day," he said. "I am Captain John Smith."

"Good day, Captain," said John Rolfe.

Pocahontas stood up.

"Why, there she is—little Pocahontas!" said Captain John Smith.

"Rebecca, do you know this man?" asked John Rolfe.

"Oh, she knows me," said Captain John Smith. "I knew you were in England, Pocahontas. Someone told me months ago, and I wanted to see you, but I had my work—so many plans. Yesterday I was passing through London, and I heard you were here."

She turned away from him. She ran off into the bedroom.

She heard Captain John Smith say, "This is odd. She knew me well in Virginia."

Pocahontas was trembling. John Smith was not dead! All the time he had been alive, and he had sent her no word.

For months he had known she was in England, yet he had not come to see her. If he had not been passing through London, he would not have stopped here today.

She had been a sister to him. She would have given her life to save his. But once he was gone from Virginia, he had forgotten her.

John Rolfe came to the door. "Rebecca," he said, "if you know this man, speak to him."

She went out into the room where John Smith was waiting. She bowed to him. "I believed you were dead," she said.

"Was it Tom Savage who told you?" he asked.

"Yes," she said.

"He saw my wound. He was sure I could not live for long," he said, "but you can see how wrong he was."

"You were alive and did not let me know," she said.

"I was so far away," he said. "For all I knew, you had forgotten me."

"You thought I could forget?" she said. "Then you never knew me, Captain John Smith."

"Pocahontas, you must not be angry." He put out his hand. "Let us talk together as we used to. I have much to say."

"Excuse me," she said.

"My wife has not been well," said John Rolfe.

She carried Thomas into the bedroom. She put him to bed and lay down beside him.

The men were talking. After a long time she heard Captain John Smith's big boots on the stairs.

He is gone, she thought. I shall never see him again.

26

✙✙✙ *GRAVESEND* ✙✙✙

The winter was long. In March there were still drifts of snow outside the inn.

Pocahontas hardly left her bed. Her cheeks were thin. Her eyes were bright with fever.

She asked John Rolfe, "Can we go home?"

"Yes," he answered.

"Can we go soon?" she asked.

"Yes, Rebecca," he said. "Captain Argall is sailing to Virginia. There are places for us on his ship."

Captain Argall came to the inn. "We sail from London a week from today," he said. "We stop at Gravesend for a load of grain. Meet us there."

John Rolfe told Pocahontas what the captain had said.

"Where is Gravesend?" she asked.

"Not far," he told her. "We can go there the night before and be ready."

They took a carriage to the town of Gravesend. They found a room over a tavern.

From below they could hear music. Someone was playing a fiddle, and a girl was singing.

"Do you mind the noise?" he asked. "Shall I ask them to be quiet?"

Pocahontas lay on the bed with her eyes closed. She was so still that he grew frightened.

He ran downstairs. "A doctor!" he said.

Someone called a doctor. He came up to the room. He bent over Pocahontas and felt her pulse and listened to her breathing.

"She is very ill," he said.

Women came from the tavern.

"The child should not be here," one of them said, and she took Thomas away.

The doctor lifted Pocahontas in bed. He gave her medicine with wine and broth.

Her eyes opened.

"Rebecca," said John Rolfe.

She looked at him as if the name meant nothing.

"Pocahontas!" he said.

She was dreaming. She heard someone speak her name, and the voice became part of her dream. It was her brother, she thought. Nantaquas was calling her. She began to run. Deep in the woods she found him. He was watching an eagle with its feet caught in a snare. The bird's eyes were fierce and proud.

She said, "Let the bird go free, Nantaquas."

John Rolfe heard her voice. "Pocahontas?" he said.

There was no answer. She would never answer him again.

He knelt by the bed and covered his face with his hands.